# Cool Characters for Kids
# 71 One-Minute Monologues

A Smith and Kraus Book
Published by Smith and Kraus, Inc.
177 Lyme Road, Hanover, NH 03755

First Edition: April 2002
Manufactured in the United States of America
10 9 8 7 6 5 4 3 2 1

*Cover design by Alex B. Karan*
*Text design by Julia Gignoux, Freedom Hill Design*

Library of Congress Cataloging-in-Publication Data
Milstein, Janet B.
Cool characters for kids : 71 one-minute monologues /
by Janet B. Milstein.
p. cm. — (Young actors series)
Summary: a collection of original monologues for elementary and
high school students to use in auditions and competitions, intended
to reflect the complex world of today.
ISBN 1-57525-306-2
1. Monologues—Juvenile literature. 2. Acting—Juvenile literature.
[1. Monologues. 2. Acting.] I. Title. II. Young actors series.
PN2080 .M467 2001
812'.6—dc21      2001049577

# Cool Characters for Kids

## 71 One-Minute Monologues
## Ages 4–12

by Janet B. Milstein

YOUNG ACTORS SERIES

A Smith and Kraus Book

# SPECIAL THANKS

I would like to express my deepest gratitude to Eric Kraus, Marisa Smith, Barbara J. Lhota, Alex B. Karan, and Karen Milstein. Without their expertise, generosity, and patience this book would not exist.

# ACKNOWLEDGMENTS

I would also like to thank the following people for their inspiration, talent, support, and trust:

Tom Anderson
Ashley Antionetti
Marianah Bardney
Shayna Bell
Lizzy Bensfield
Brianna Blessing
Charles Braboy
Mitch Bretall
Michael Brown
Adam Budz
Chris Budz
Lindsey Bugno
Megan Calvert
Clover Campbell
Lizette Casas
Evelyn Chen
Vince Chiarelli
Adrian Collier
Christina Collins
Victoria Collins
Ellen Crabill
Miss Crabill's 3rd
   Grade Class at Ray
   School
David Croom
Anthony Evola
Brittani Franklin
Maya Franklin
Lauren Frost
Adrian Garcia

Brianna Garcia
Mercades Garcia
Emily Gifford
Jennifer Gifford
Julia Hill Gignoux
Alisa Grin
Lily Hanscom
Matt Hanscom
Allison Hart
Wendy Hart
Lily Ho
Jane Hoffman
Irene Ingold
Claude Johnson Jr.
Patrick Johnson
Vince Karczynski
Lauren Kirby
Katya Kobzeva
George Korchev
Amanda Kwiatkowski
Debbie Lamedman
Nicholas Lanas
Millie Larson
Cassie Leja
Erin Mary
John Miller
Amethyst Milstein
Donald Milstein
Freda Milstein
Joshua Milstein

Karen L. Milstein
Karen S. Milstein
Kathryn Milstein
Melissa Milstein
Natalie Milstein
Peggy Milstein
Elizabeth Monteleone
Morgan Moore
Zoe Moritz
Freddy Munoz
Francielle Murray
Miranda Palmer
Malika Paracha
Alexandria Poddebniak
Rohana Radhakrishnan
Sierra Rhodes
Jessica Robbins
Curtis Rowe
Lisa Ruszkowski
Samuel Sohn
Elizabeth Soloveva
Katie Ann Srebalus
Marcella Unate
Anton Urusov
Angela Ventrella
Heather Washburn
Jennifer White
Ebboney Wilson
Shalyn Wismer

# Contents

## BOYS' COMIC MONOLOGUES

## BOYS' DRAMATIC MONOLOGUES

## GIRLS' OR BOYS' COMIC MONOLOGUES

## GIRLS' OR BOYS' DRAMATIC MONOLOGUES

*This book is dedicated to my amazing niece, Amethyst.*

# Foreword

Kids and acting. Who can think of a more potent combination for truthful, unpredictable, outrageous fun? Working with young actors is exciting and refreshing, but it can also be chaotic. Yet it is out of the chaos and abundant energy of my students that the characters in this book emerged.

When my young students needed monologues for auditions and competitions, I sent them in search of material. What they brought back were monologues written in kids' voices, but lacking in motivation. The characters seemed to be delivering speeches or reflecting on life, without having something to fight for. In short, they lacked purpose. The material also underestimated my students' capabilities, especially when it came to dramatic monologues. I knew they could handle more challenging material and simply could not allow them to perform pieces that didn't do them justice. My solution? To write monologues for my students that were as funny, touching, complex and unique as they were. That became my challenge, privilege and, ultimately, this book.

Working with the new material, my students achieved astounding results. The more reserved children came out of their shells and the livelier kids channeled their energy into their performances. The students were truly enjoying themselves because they could relate to the characters and the situations in the monologues. They understood what they wanted from the "invisible other character" and went for it, free of inhibition, as kids do in life. As a result, their personalities shone through, their confidence increased, and their acting improved dramatically. I was so excited and moved that I made up my mind to offer the monologues to other young children in the hopes of achieving similar results.

The monologues are new, but they've been put to the test. Agents, managers, directors, and the harshest critics of all — kids — have approved! My students have performed many of the pieces at the International Model and Talent Association conventions in New York and Los Angeles, as well as for agents and directors in various audition situations. Some have won monologue awards, some have received callbacks, some have gotten agency representation. All have had fun and have felt proud of their performances.

Now it's your turn. The material within these pages is perfect for auditions, drama classes, speech improvement, or just plain fun! I hope you have as good a time working on them as I had working with the "real" cool kids who inspired them. Break a leg!

*Janet B. Milstein*

# How to Use This Book

When writing this book, I tried to make it as kid-friendly as possible, so I hope you find it easy to use. The monologues are one minute and under — perfect for a young child's memorization capabilities and most audition situations. The book is divided into girls' monologues, boys' monologues, and girls' or boys' monologues. These sections are then subdivided into comic and dramatic categories for easy searching. The pieces are designed for kids aged four to twelve. However, since children mature and develop verbal skills at their own pace, the characters' ages are not indicated. For your convenience, I have arranged the monologues in each section from youngest to oldest. A brief description of the situation precedes each monologue and quickly sets the scene.

Often you will see *(Beat.)* within the text. A beat is a pause and is usually included to indicate that the "invisible other character" is speaking. However, a beat is occasionally taken simply because the character paused. Either way, it is up to the actor to figure out what happened during each beat and to keep those moments alive. What did the other character say or do? Look at the surrounding lines for clues. Make clear, creative choices that make sense under the given circumstances. Taking the time to *hear* their words and *see* their actions makes for a more genuine performance.

And finally, when selecting monologues for auditions, be sure to consider the nature of the material as well as the child's maturity level, age and casting range; portraying a character for which the child could realistically be cast will increase his or her chances of getting a callback. And that's the next big step toward landing the part!

# Girls'
# Comic Monologues

# CANDYLAND

**Comic**

*Kaitlyn has just returned from Toys R Us with her mom and is talking to her grandmother.*

**Kaitlyn:** Grandma, can I have a snack? Please?! I'm so hungry cause Mom took me to Toys R Us. She said I could pick out one game. Anything I wanted in the whole store! So I looked and looked, and then I found Candyland. I saw the gum drops and the ice cream floats — I was so excited to eat all the candy! But I tasted it, and it all just tastes like cardboard. *(Makes a yucky face.)* I guess I must have picked a spoiled box.

# THE WARDROBE

Comic

*Katie has accidentally discovered a way to get her mom to buy her new clothes. Here, she shares her secret with a good friend.*

**Katie:** Last week my mom bought me chocolate ice cream while she shopped in the mall! It taste so good that I licked it real hard and it fell on my yellow shirt. I started to cry cause it was all messy and cold, so my mom bought me a new pink shirt. Then we were driving to my best friend's birthday party, and by accident I spilled my Juicy-Juice all over my white dress! Even my mom couldn't wipe the purple stains out. I felt so bad, I started crying! So my mom stopped at the store and bought me a pretty red dress. I figure, if I keep spilling my food, by next month I'll have a brand new wardrobe!!

Award winner: Comedy Monologue Competition, International Modeling & Talent Association, New York 1998 Convention.

# THE SCHOOL DANCE

Comic

*Cindy's older sister, Diana, left for the big school dance earlier this evening. Cindy asks her mom about getting older.*

**Cindy:** Mommy, when I get older can I go to the school dance like Diana did tonight? *(Beat.)* And will I get to wear a pretty dress and drink punch? *(Beat.)* I can't wait! I love to dress up. But I don't want to kiss boys, because I think that's gross. Unless it's Kenny Brown. He's so cute, I'd kiss him four times! *(Beat.)* Mommy, what does spike mean? *(Beat.)* Yeah, spike. Diana said they were gonna spike the punch. *(Beat.)* Mommy, where are you going?!

# MARRYING MATTHEW

Comic

*Tammy can't wait to tell her dad about her exciting day and her big plans for the future.*

**Tammy:** Daddy, Daddy! Guess what? Matthew proposed to me today! *(Beat.)* Matthew — he's my boyfriend. Now we're gonna get married like you and Mommy. And you know how you gave Mommy her ring? Well, Matthew's gonna give me one too! Only mine's gonna have a *big* diamond in it, not a tiny one like Mommy's. And we're gonna get our own house! But he's gonna have to sleep in his own room cause he snores like a monster — just like you do. Oh, and ya wanna know the best part? Miss Rich told me since I'm the bride and you're my dad, you get to pay for the wedding!

# WHOOPS!

Comic

*Maya was just asked if she could come out to play. Here, she explains to her friend, Candice, why she's not allowed.*

**Maya:** I can't come out today, Candice. 'Cause this morning when I was getting ready for school, my brother started teasing me and pulling my hair. I screamed so loud that my dad came busting into the room and said, "If you two don't keep it down I'm going to whoop your butts." Then my brother goes, "It's her fault. She's the one who should get whooped." My dad yelled, "Don't you tell me what to do! You're staying in today. You better come home right after school." I couldn't help it — I started to laugh. So my dad said, "You think that's funny? Well, you're staying in too. No going out to play with your friends." He's so grouchy when we wake him up. Hey! He never said I couldn't have my friends come *in. (Beat.)* No, he's not gonna whoop your butt. He just says that. It's my mom who does the whooping around here. And she's not home!

Award winner: Comedy Monologue Competition, International Modeling & Talent Association, Los Angeles 2000 Convention.

# COLOR-FREE

Serio-Comic

*Ame just got home from school. She can't wait to tell her aunt that her advice worked.*

**Ame:** Aunt Karen, Aunt Karen, it worked! Miss Cheryl made us draw a tree in Art class today. She drew one for us to copy. It was all green and brown at the bottom and I thought that was really ugly. So I made my tree pink and blue with pretty purple birds. When she saw it, she yelled, "That's all wrong! There are no such things as pink trees!" So I said what you told me to say if she picked on me again. I said, "Art is about imagination and you are a bad art teacher to try and stunt up my creativity." All the kids started clapping and she turned bright red. So she took me to the Principal's office and told him what I said. And he said I was right and that she better change her altitude or something. And then he told the class we could use any colors we want! So we all made a big tree with every color in the rainbow! And it's for you.

# THE GOOD GIRL

Comic

*Heather is shocked that she didn't get everything she wanted from Santa, but her best friend did. Heather tries to win her friend's sympathy.*

**Heather:** You're lucky. Santa totally gypped me this year. I only had twelve things on my Christmas list. That's all. You should see how many presents I get from my mom and dad on my birthday! Santa only gave me nine. Nine! I got all the games I asked for, but he left out the computer, the merry-go-round for the backyard, and the pony! Those were the things I wanted most! And I was so good all year 'cause I knew. . .Oh, no! I bet it's because I pulled Suzy Dawson's hair when she called me stupid! *(Beat.)* She better not have got a pony.

Award winner: Comedy Monologue Competition, International Modeling & Talent Association, Los Angeles 2001 Convention.

# THE MAID AND MISS BONBON

Comic

*Lindsay's about to play the usual game with her big sister, but this time she wants to change the rules.*

**Lindsay:** How come every time we play, I have to be the maid? Why don't *you* be the maid this time and *I'll* be the rich lady? I know you're older than me, but this is make-believe. Besides, the rich lady could have a cranky, old maid. That would be perfect for you. I mean, you'd play her good. Or maybe the rich lady got rich really young because her mom and dad died and left her tons of money. That would be so sad. She wouldn't be any fun to play then. But you know what? I'd do her part, just so you wouldn't have to. *(Beat.)* Oh, c'mon! *(Beat.)* Okay, okay, fine! Let's play. *(In her maid's voice.)* Miss BonBon? I'm sorry to bother you when you're counting your money. But I have some very important news for you. *(Beat.)* I quit and I want my paycheck in cash!

Award winner: Comedy Monologue Competition, International Modeling & Talent Association, New York 2001 Convention.

# STICKS AND STONES

Comic

*Lisa finally outsmarted her brother today and is eager to impress her friend with how she did it.*

**Lisa:** My brother thinks he's so smart. He's always showing off and making fun of me. If I make the tiniest mistake he calls me names like dummy or moron or bozo-brain. Yesterday he came up to me and said, "What is nine and nine?" I said, "eighteen." And he laughed and said, "It's ninety-nine, dummy!" I was so mad! I hate when he calls me that. Then he goes, "Ask me a question, bozo. Come on! Can't you think of any?" So I thought for a minute and then I said, "Why is the sky blue? How come birds can fly? Why does the President have so many girlfriends?" He just stood there all quiet, staring at me. Then he goes, "You think you're so smart, don't you?" I said, "No, I don't think so. I know so!"

Award winner: Comedy Monologue Competition, International Modeling & Talent Association, Los Angeles 2001 Convention.

# THE TOOTH FAIRY

Comic

*Mandy helps her little sister learn what is true and what is make-believe.*

**Mandy:** *Fairy Tale* was a movie! There's no such thing as real fairies. Think about it. If they existed, we'd see them caught in our bug zapper. Or we'd feel them get squashed under our bare feet in the grass. If you can't see them or feel them, they don't exist. That's why the only fairy that is real is the Tooth Fairy. I know that for a fact because she leaves me cold, hard cash. Now that's something you can feel.

# MY OWN ROOM

Comic

*Cassie is about to learn to be careful what she asks for...because she just might get it.*

**Cassie:** Dad, just hear me out. I want my own room. You promised a long time ago. Nobody ever uses the guest room downstairs. We never have any guests. I've been sharing a room with Jill for 3 years now. I need privacy. I need more space. I want to be able to talk to my friends without her listening in and do my homework without her bugging me to play with her. I'm responsible. I'm all grown up now. She still sleeps with her Snoopy night-light on. She's messy. She snores. She's making my life miserable! She's. . .what? I can? I can have the guest room?! Oh, thank you! I love you so much! Wow, I'll have the whole huge room all to myself. That gigantic room downstairs with no one but me. *(Realizing she'll be scared all alone.)* Daddy? Can Jill sleep in my room tonight?

# SQUISHY LOCKERS

Comic

*Catherine tries to convince the school principal that the students' lockers need to be bigger.*

**Catherine:** Mr. Saler, I need to talk to you since you're the principal and this is very important. Our lockers are way too small. Every time I stuff my coat in, I'm scared it won't ever squeeze back out. I put my Chia Pet in my locker and he sprouted major hair and now he's jammed. If I scrape him out, he'll lose his hair. And he's ugly when he's bald. And now we're gonna be part of "Read Across America." Miss Miller told us to put books and pillows in our lockers to read later in the hallway. We can't fit pillows in our puny lockers! Maybe a pillow*case*. An open book is bigger than my locker door. How am I gonna read across America when I can't even read across my locker? Look, you know Dana Ford, right? She's the teeniest girl in my class and even *she* can't fit in her locker. We just tested. And now she's stuck with only one leg in! One leg! This is all your fault. Now what are you gonna do about it?

# ROLE CALL

Comic

*Star just found out she didn't get the role she wanted in the school play — her best friend did. Upset, she tries to scare her friend out of playing the role.*

**Star:** You got the role? You got cast as Annie? That role was mine. I'm perfect for it. What did I get? *(Beat.)* Understudy?! For you?! You've got to be kidding me! You can't even sing. I'm just telling you so you won't embarrass yourself in front of everyone. And you know that song, *(She sings.)* "The sun will come out, tomorrow"? That means the sun's *not* out. It will be rainy and cloudy and gloomy the whole time you work on the show! Plus, that woman is gonna be so mean to you because you're an orphan. And you don't even get a cat. Just a big, old, ugly dog! Gosh, I feel so bad for you. *(Beat.)* What? Will I do it for you? I don't know, it's a pretty pathetic role. *(Beat.)* Okay, okay, I'll do it. But only because you're my best friend.

Award winner: Comedy Monologue Competition, International Modeling & Talent Association, Los Angeles 2000 & 2001 Conventions.

# TOMBOYS RULE

Comic

*Robin is a great basketball player and tall for her age. Her coach has just surprised her by telling her to play against an older boy, Tyler. Robin doesn't want to play him, but not because she thinks she'll lose.*

**Robin:** No way, coach! It's not fair. He's a boy. You really expect me to play him one-on-one? Plus he's older than me and all his friends will be watching. It's just not right, coach. *(Beat.)* I'll whip his butt. Then he'll be totally embarrassed because, one — he's a boy, and, two — he's an *older* boy. Plus boys always think they're all that. When I win he'll end up running home to cry. *(Beat.)* Oh really, Tyler? You think you can beat me? Fine, you want to play? Bring it on! Get ready because I'm gonna crush you like a bug — short stuff!

# THE STAR CHART

Comic

*Jenna really doesn't feel like doing her chores tonight, so she decides to trick her little sister into doing them for her.*

**Jenna:** Julie, see this chart? It's a list of chores that Mom made. It says, "make bed, set the table, clean room." Each time I do one of these things, Mom gives me a star. A shiny star! A beautiful star! Sometimes even gold! Look over here. There's my name and — hey! You're name isn't on here at all! Oh no! That means you can never, ever, ever get any stars! That's not fair. I bet you'd love lots of pretty stars, wouldn't you? Mom must think you're too young to earn stars. Hey! I have an idea to help you out, Julie. I'll make a chart like this with *your* name on it and keep it under your pillow. Then every time you clean up my room or make my bed, I'll give you *three* stars! I'll feel kinda sad to only get one measly star from Mom, but I'll do it 'cause I know it will make you happy. Want some cool silver stars right now?! Okay — go set the table.

Award winner: Comedy Monologue Competition, International Modeling & Talent Association, New York 1998 Convention.

# BOYS ARE MADE FOR BOSSING

Comic

*Shannon helps Brian ask her to the dance.*

**Shannon:** Brian, did you hear about the stupid dance next week? Who ever came up with the idea that having a dance in the school gym is fun? You're going, right? *(Beat.)* Me too. Well, since it's gonna be so boring, I was thinking you should come sit by me so we can talk and stuff. Ya know, just so we don't fall asleep. And if they actually play something good I'll even let you dance with me. And you should wear your really cool black jacket so in case I get cold you can let me wear it. Plus don't forget to bring enough money to buy me snacks, okay? Oh, and just in case you get embarrassed easily, I promise not to tell anyone that you asked me to the dance.

# BRIGHT LIGHTS AND PEARLY WHITES

Comic

*Lily really wants a make-up mirror with lights so she can look closely at her reflection. Or does she?*

**Lily:** You know how bad I've wanted that make-up mirror with the lights, right? I mean, you have one and so does Missy and Jen and Kelly. Well, I saved twenty dollars that I got for my birthday, but I still needed five more. I was racking my brains, trying to figure out how I could get the rest. Then it dawned on me! I had a couple of loose teeth and my mom gives me $1.50 for each tooth. So I got some taffy and stuffed a big glob of it in my mouth. And it worked! One of my teeth fell out! So I kept chewing and chewing, and before I knew it, all *four* loose teeth came out! My mom gave me six dollars and I ran to the store and bought the make-up mirror. I was so excited! But when I got home and looked in it with those bright lights, my mouth looked like the Grand Canyon! I'm never smiling again! Now, will you please come with me to return the stupid mirror?

# Girls'
# Dramatic Monologues

# THE EMPTY FISH BOWL

Dramatic

*Amber just got to school and has to tell her teacher what happened to the class pet last night.*

**Amber:** Miss Jenson? I know I was supposed to bring Goldie back today, but. . .um. . .Well, me and my dad put his fish bowl on my desk in my room. And I fed him just a pinch of food like you showed me and I watched him swim around until I had to go to bed. Well, this morning I woke up and Goldie was gone from his bowl! So I called my dad and he looked all over my room and then. . .he found a small piece of his tail. My cat Toby killed him and it's all my fault! I should have closed the door! I should have locked Toby out! I didn't mean for it to happen. I didn't mean for him to die. *(Beat.)* Miss Jenson, do you think Goldie went to Heaven?

# SANTA'S SECRET HELPER

**Dramatic**

*Becky is about to ask Santa for the most important gift she's ever wanted.*

**Becky:** Santa? I hope you can hear me 'cause I was coloring with my new markers, so I don't have any paper left. I already wrote you a letter saying that I want new Barbies and a magic set and some pretty purple clothes, instead of those itchy, hot sweaters Aunt Millie keeps giving me. I'm sure you got it by now. But I hope it's not too late, 'cause I wanna change my Christmas list. I don't want any toys or any clothes. I just want one thing. Santa? Can you please make Mommy and Daddy stop yelling at each other? They fight all the time and it always makes me cry. Can you please make them happy again? That's all I want for Christmas. I promise I'll be really good. I love you, Santa. Thank you.

Award winner: Drama Monologue Competition, International Modeling & Talent Association, Los Angeles 2000 Convention.

# A PLACE CALLED HEAVEN

Dramatic

*Danni's mom has been very sick and got home last night from the hospital. This morning, Danni creeps into her room to see if she's okay.*

**Danni:** Mommy? Are you awake? What happened to your hair?! It was there when you came home from the hospital yesterday. *(Beat.)* A wig?! Daddy told me the doctors had to cut some off, but why'd they take it all? It's scaring me. Will it grow back? *(Beat.)* Well, maybe you can get lots of pretty wigs and I'll brush them for you. I'm so glad you're home. I missed you. Daddy can't cook very good. But I got to eat lots of pizza. Daddy said the doctors didn't make you all better. Maybe me and Daddy can make you chicken soup like you make when I'm sick. And then you'll get better and we can go to the playground and Chuck E. Cheese and — *(Beat.)* Why not? *(Beat.)* Where are you going? To a new hospital? *(Beat.)* Heaven? Will you come back? *(Beat.)* Mommy, no! I don't want you to go there! Don't leave! Stay with me. I love you, Mommy. Please promise you won't go away.

Award winner: Drama Monologue Competition, International Modeling & Talent Association, Los Angeles 2000 Convention.

# LOSING MISTY

Dramatic

*Anna's cat, Misty, has been sick for days. When Anna looks for Misty under the bed this morning, she isn't there. Anna is happy that the cat isn't sleeping anymore and asks her mom if she knows where Misty is.*

**Anna:** Mommy, guess what?! Misty isn't under my bed! You know how she's been lying in that same spot all the time. So she must be feeling better! Did you see where she went? *(Beat.)* Asleep? Again?! God, she sleeps more than babies do. Where is she sleeping? *(Beat.)* At the doctor's?! Oh, no! Is she sick again, Mommy? 'Cause if she is, I want to go pet her. She doesn't like the doctor. He scares her. Can we go visit her please? *(Beat.)* So what if the doctor put her to sleep. We can bring her some cat food and wake her up *(Beat.)* Forever? You mean she can never wake up? *(Beat.)* No, Mommy, that's not true! I can wake her up! I know I can — I know it! She loves me! Let's go there now. Mommy, please!! I want Misty back! She can't die, Mommy! She can't.

Award winner: Drama Monologue Competition, International Modeling & Talent Association, Los Angeles 2000 Convention.

# THE FISHING PARTNER

## Dramatic

*Amanda doesn't want to go fishing with her dad anymore. Even though she's nervous, she decides she has to tell him.*

**Amanda:** Daddy? I know we're supposed to go fishing today, but. . .I don't want to go. *(Beat.)* Because last week, remember how I caught that big Bonito? I was so excited. But then, I watched it flopping around in the huge bucket. I couldn't stop staring at it. It was trying so hard to breathe — to stay alive. And I sat there and watched it die. It was the saddest thing I ever saw. I felt so bad for killing it. It's not like we even ate it. You gave it to the neighbors. I didn't say anything that day, because I knew you were so proud of me and. . .I know you really wanted a boy. I'm sorry you got stuck with me. If I was a boy I probably wouldn't care, and then you'd still have a fishing partner. I'm so sorry! Daddy? Do you still love me?

Award winner: Drama Monologue Competition, International Modeling & Talent Association, Los Angeles 2000 Convention.

# NIGHTTIME ACCIDENTS

**Dramatic**

*Chrissy is getting ready to go to a sleep-over party at her friend Valerie's house. Chrissy wants to go but she's afraid, so she tries to convince her mom to let her stay home.*

**Chrissy:** Yes I'm ready Mom, but I don't really want to go. It's just a boring sleep-over party. Can't I stay home instead? *(Beat.)* I know we already bought Valerie a present, but I could give it to her tomorrow or in school. Besides, I think Blackie will be lonely without me here. *(Beat.)* But Mom! I can't go — please?! I'm afraid I might wet the bed! Then everyone will know and they'll all laugh at me. And what if I wet through the sleeping bag onto their rug? Her mom and dad will get so mad at me. And everyone will say, "gross," and they'll never want me to sleep over ever, ever again. *(Beat.)* I *do* want to go to the party but. . .Mom, do you think you can pick me up before bedtime and say I'm not allowed to spend the night? Please?

# PLAYING FAVORITES

Dramatic

*Beth's mom (or dad) just got back from a business trip with presents for her and her sister. Beth tells her (or him) she hates the gift, but what she really hates is not feeling special anymore.*

**Beth:** I hate it. It's ugly. How come I get the retarded walrus and Kyra gets the unicorn? The unicorn's beautiful and way more cool. You always do that. Remember how you got us T-shirts when you went to Florida? Kyra got the purple one with the sparkly seashells. I got the stupid orange one with a boat. Like who wants to wear that? And she told me you took her to the mall when I was at Vicky's house. Why didn't you ask if I wanted to go? You used to do stuff with me, now it's just Kyra all the time. You love her more than me, don't you? She's your favorite. I thought *I* was. You used to say I was your little sweetheart. But not to tell anyone because they'd be jealous. Why did you lie to me? Why?

# FITTING IN

**Dramatic**

*Heidi doesn't like school very much these days. In an attempt to avoid going, she tells her mom what's been going on.*

**Heidi:** Can I stay home with you today, Mom? I don't want to go to school. I hate it. I don't ever wanna go back. *(Beat.)* Because there are these two girls, Lori and Daria, and they always make fun of me. Lori came up to me and said, "We counted and you wore those same pants four days in a row! That's disgusting!" And Daria said, "I bet it's because you can't fit into any other clothes!" They always laugh at me and make me feel embarrassed and fat. I hate them. Why are they so mean to me? I didn't do anything to them. When they're alone they're kinda nice, but as soon as they're together they start acting like they're so cool and teasing me. Maybe they're right. Maybe I'm too fat for anybody to like me. I'm gonna go on a diet right away. And I better throw away those pants. They're my favorites, but. . .I don't want to be picked on anymore.

# MISSING BARBIE

**Dramatic**

*Jane and Barbie have been best friends for years, but lately, Jane feels like Barbie is deserting her. Barbie has just called and Jane's older sister, who is visiting, answers the phone. Jane refuses to talk to Barbie.*

**Jane:** Hang up the phone. I don't want to talk to her. *(Beat.)* Because Barbie is so mean. She was my best friend. She told me she liked me better than anyone in the whole world. We always did everything together. Built sand castles at the beach, played games, watched movies, played catch. Now she has a new friend, Linda. I even introduced them. And since then, Barbie spends all her time with Linda, not me. When she *is* around, all she does is talk about Linda — Linda this and Linda that. I can tell she doesn't really want to hang out with me because she'd much rather be with her new friend. God, I hate her! How could she just stop hanging out with me and leave me all by myself? She was my best friend ever. I miss her. I want her back, like we were before.

# SCIENCE WITH CHARLIE

Dramatic

*In science class, Mr. Thorton tells the students their pet hamster, Charlie, has died. Amy is really upset because she knows how it happened. After class, she admits what she knows to the teacher.*

**Amy:** Mr. Thorton? I need to talk to you about the hamster. But promise me you won't say anything to Debbie Snyder? *(Beat.)* Well, yesterday after class, Debbie realized she left her notebook in here, so I came back with her to get it. And she saw Charlie running around in his cage and she got this idea. She thought it would be funny to put him in your desk drawer so you'd open it and get shocked. I told her not to, but she did it anyway and shut the drawer. I was scared he might get hurt, so we opened the drawer and he was gone! We didn't know where he went. Then we opened the drawer under it and he was in there. He must have fallen when she pulled the top drawer open cause his nose was all bloody and scraped up and. . .when you announced today that he died, I. . .it was our fault! We killed him! It was an accident. But he's dead, and no matter how horrible I feel, I can never bring him back to life. I'm so sorry! I didn't mean it! I didn't.

Award winner: Drama Monologue Competition, International Modeling & Talent Association, Los Angeles 2000 Convention.

# MOM, COME HOME

**Dramatic**

*Marissa's mom has been sick for over a month, so Marissa has been in charge of keeping the house clean. When her little sister has an accident, Marissa can't help yelling at her.*

**Marissa:** Jessica, what did you do?! Look at this mess you made! You better clean it up now. There's going to be paint stuck on the carpet! Why can't you think before you do stupid things?! *(Beat.)* Jess, I'm sorry. Please don't cry. I didn't mean to yell at you. It's just that with Mom in the hospital, I'm supposed to take care of things and it's hard. I'm not a grown-up, but I have to try to be because Dad has to work extra hard to pay for Mom's hospital bills. But everything's going to be okay. Mom will get better and come home and it'll be just like it used to. I know it. *(Beat.)* How about I help you clean this up — we'll do it together. I love you, Jess. Will you give me a hug?

# PROTECTING SARAH

*Yesterday, Jacky's younger sister, Sarah, came home from school crying. When Jacky asked what was wrong, Sarah finally admitted that Danielle, a girl from school, was making fun of her. Today, Jacky confronts Danielle.*

**Jacky:** You're Danielle, right? I thought so. I'm Sarah's sister Jacky. You know, Sarah Morton? Yeah, I'm sure you do because she came home crying yesterday. She told me that you were calling her names in front of all your friends. *(Beat.)* Oh, you weren't, huh? That's weird because my sister never lies. In fact, I had to drag it out of her. So I suggest you think again before saying it wasn't you. And I also suggest that you listen very carefully. If you ever, ever, bother my sister again, I promise you, you'll wish you were never born. You got that? Good. Don't forget, Danielle. Because I guarantee you I won't.

# LOOK MY WAY

**Dramatic**

*Fran has had a big crush on Justin for the entire school year. Tonight at the skating rink, Fran sees Justin skating with Ashley. She is so upset that she goes outside to cry. A few minutes later, Justin comes outside. Fran quickly wipes her eyes.*

**Fran:** Oh — hey — hi Justin. I just came out here for some air, ya know? Sometimes they play the music so loud and it gets hot and stuffy when everyone's skating. I saw you skating with Ashley. You looked like you were having fun. *(Beat.)* Well, I think I'm gonna go home now. *(Beat.)* What do you *think* is wrong?! You're with a girl I can't stand and you're the one. . . Forget it — never mind. I gotta go. *(Beat.)* What?! God, don't you get it? I've liked you for such a long time. You never even noticed. Do you have any idea how bad that makes me feel? And what do you do? You go and skate with Ashley, when she doesn't even like you and talks behind your back. But I don't care because I don't like you anymore. *(She starts to cry.)* I changed my mind. And don't say I'm crying because I'm not. I would never cry about someone as stupid as you.

# Boys'
# Comic Monologues

# PICK ME!

**Comic**

*In class, David desperately begs his teacher to pick him first.*

**David:** Ooh, ooh, ooh! Here! Pick me! I wanna go first! Pleeeease! *(Yelling.)* Miss Janet, can you hear me?? Meee, go, first! Hey, c'mon! What do I gotta do to get noticed around here? *(Jumping on each word.)* Pick me, not Nick. He's gonna get sick! *(Stops jumping.)* Well, he always does. Barf, barf, barf! *(Beat.)* Okay, I'm being good. See? *(Sits down, hands folded.)* I'm quiet. Hey Miss Janet, I'm being really quiet. Look how quiet I am! I'm as quiet as a mouse. Quieter, 'cause mice squeak. I'm quiet like a bug. They don't talk at all. Miss Janet, you look so pretty. I like your dress. And you have nice hair like my mom's — brown and gray. So can I go? Please? *(Beat.)* Wow, I can?! Yes! Cool! Woo! Hey. . .what were we gonna do again?

Award winner: Comedy Monologue Competition, International Modeling & Talent Association, Los Angeles 2001 Convention.

# THE SMOOTH TALKER

Comic

*Collin is determined to get a girlfriend.*

**Collin:** Christy, you're so pretty. I have a crush on you. I wanna sit next to you. I love you. Will you be my girlfriend? *(Beat.)* Don't run away! *(Beat.)* Hi Morgan. You're so pretty. I like you a lot. Do you want to be my girlfriend? *(Beat.)* Stop laughing! Come back! *(Beat.)* Hi Angela — wait! I didn't even ask yet!

# SHOW AND TELL

Comic

*Jake has a very original show and tell.*

**Jake:** For show and tell I was gonna bring my birthday cake, but we ate it all up. And I got a new bed, but I couldn't carry it here 'cause it's too big. Me and my brothers and my cousin Ted played Cowboys and Indians, Cops and Robbers, and Superheroes. So for my show and tell I brought this. . .*(Pointing to elbow.)* Here is where the cops got me. And this *(Moving hair to show his forehead.)* is where an Indian hit me with an arrow. Then there's one *(He looks at his butt.)* where I can't show you on my body. Oh, and here *(Lifting pant leg to show his knee.)* is where Superdog bit me. My uncle Vinny said that bruises make you look tough, and girls like that. *(Beat.)* Wanna see more?

# THE ALIEN

Comic

*Timmy tries to convince his mom that his messy room is not his fault.*

**Timmy:** Mom, it's not my fault my room's a mess! Me and Anthony were playing with his new race cars. Only four of them. And we heard a weird noise outside, so we opened the window. This huge spaceship landed and a slimy, green alien with three heads came out and jumped in the window. Anthony tried to shoot him with my zapper gun, but it didn't even hurt him — he just got real mad. So he knocked all the books off my shelf and picked up my toy box with his long, purple antennas and dumped it all over my room. So I threw a Frisbee at him and it bonked him on his third head and he slimed out the window and the spaceship disappeared into the sky. Geez, Mom, you should be happy I'm still alive!

# SNARFED

Comic

*Keith explains to his friend why he doesn't drink soda anymore.*

**Keith:** No, I'll have juice. I don't want to drink soda anymore. Because today I went out to lunch with my dad and my friend Brian. And we got hamburgers and fries and Cokes. And Brian said, "Did you see the man cooking our hamburgers? He looked like a hairy ape." I started laughing so hard that the soda came out my nose!! God did that hurt! Brian started cracking up and he went, "You snarfed, ha ha ha! You snarfed!" And I started laughing too and we couldn't stop. And the next thing I know, my dad started giggling too and whoosh — he snarfed too! It's kinda scary to see soda pouring out of your dad's nose. Even though it's still kinda funny. So from now on, I'm drinking juice. 'Cause I don't think you can snarf juice.

# WHAT A WASTE

Comic

*Patrick tries to convince his mom that cleaning things is a waste of time.*

**Patrick:** Mom, I don't see why I have to make my bed because when it's bedtime, I have to get in it and it just gets all wrinkled up again. And I don't think I should brush my teeth anymore because at lunchtime, I eat food and my teeth get all dirty again. Plus, why should I clean up my room when it's gonna be a mess again as soon as I come home and play? It's just a waste of cleaning. *(Beat.)* Don't play?! But Mom, it's better to have my room always messy than always clean. That way I know where everything is.

# THE GROWN-UP

Comic

*Matthew decides it's time to act grown up like his dad.*

**Matthew:** Dad, can I borrow your razor? *(Beat.)* Because I finally grew a mustache today. Look. *(Beat.)* Well look closer, it's there. I can see it. And I have to shave it off right away or I'll never get a girlfriend. It'll look stupid and get food stuck in it. Besides, girls don't like mustaches cause it feels gross when you kiss them. *(Beat.)* Lisa Rosen told me. Dad, you're going to have to face the fact that I'm all grown up. I'm a man now, and I have to start doing grown-up things like you do. Like shaving and wearing cologne and showering on a regular basis. *(Beat.)* Mow the lawn? Hey, look! My mustache was just a fuzz from the blanket. I guess I don't have to shave after all!

Award winner: Comedy Monologue Competition, International Modeling & Talent Association, New York 2001 Convention.

# NOT MEDICINE!

Comic

*Poor Chas is sick but he'd rather pretend he's well than take his awful medicine.*

**Chas:** Mom, I feel so much better! Suddenly I don't feel sick anymore. I think I can go to school now. I know it's strange but maybe my stomach got all better when I burped. Look I can jump up and down and I'm not dizzy at all. *(He's kind of dizzy.)* Mom I don't need that medicine! Please! I'm not sick, okay? I never felt so good in my whole life! I can't wait to get to school. I wanna learn. I love my teachers. I can't wait to make a paper Eskimo. Mom! Put the medicine away! What if I'm allergic to it, and I fall down and curl up on the floor, and my eyes go in circles, and oozy, green gunk comes out of my mouth and nose and eyes? *(Beat.)* But Mom! I feel so — *(She shoves a spoonful of medicine in his mouth.)* Mmm, cherry! Can I have some more?

# LET 'EM RIP

Comic

*Todd urges his mom to stop wearing pantyhose because they always rip.*

**Todd:** See, Mom! I told you not to put them on! Your pantyhose always rip. Now I'm going to be late for school again. I don't know why you wear them in the first place. They make your toes look like duck feet. And it's not like you buy them in cool colors like purple or silver. They're the same color as your legs, so what's the point? Plus it takes you forever to get them on. You look like a crazy ballerina doing all those bends and kicks, trying to squeeze into them. Your face gets all red and sweaty just trying to get them all the way up. And after all that work, you always get a rip. Remember when my new red shirt ripped that one time and you went back to the store and waited in line to return it? Well, if you took back every pair of ripped pantyhose you own, you'd have to *live* in that store! Are you ready yet? *(Beat. Her new pantyhose rip.)* Oh, no!

# FISHING WITH DAD

Comic

*Michael tells his friend, Steven, why he will never go fishing again.*

**Michael:** Hey, Steven! You won't believe what happened to me today! You know my dad's a police officer, right? Well, he had a day off of work today and he finally took me fishing. We went out in a boat on the lake, right? And we're waiting and waiting when suddenly, I got a big bite! And then my dad got one too. My fish was almost bending my rod in half and my dad couldn't help me because he was reeling in *his* fish. My fish was so strong that suddenly it pulled me into the water! The next thing I know, my dad grabbed me and helped me back into the boat. And he was holding his gun, looking to shoot the fish! I was scared to death! Well, he couldn't see it anywhere so he grabbed his rod and reeled it in, and ya know what he caught? *My* rod! Our fishing lines were tangled together in a big knot! There never was a fish! It was my dad who yanked me into the lake! My own dad! I'm never going fishing again!

# TOP-SECRET MISSION

Comic

Zachary, "Secret Agent Zalamar," convinces his cosmic brother to help him dig up his action figures.

**Zachary:** This is a top-secret mission. You must say the sacred oath to me. "As a brave secret agent, I pledge my loyalty to my cosmic brother Zalamar. Zoyt!" Okay, I snuck down to the d-e-n to scope out the activities. A strange, little, female creature was seen giving similar creatures our heroes' statues. *(Beat.)* My action figures, duh! Then the strange creatures ran to the woods and buried them beneath the earth. Our mission: to locate and save all heroic figures before dinner. *(Beat.)* Oh, c'mon! I don't wanna dig them up by myself! Zoyt! Zoyt! Fine, go home. By the way, the earth mother is ordering large quantities of pizza for this evening's fuel. *(Beat.)* You'll stay? You are a true secret agent, cosmic brother! Do you like Pepperoni?

# THE PERFECT AGE

Comic

*Andre wishes that he were older.*

**Andre:** I'm sick of being my age. I want to be older right now so I can do all kinds of cool things. Like my brother Scott. He gets to drive and stay up late and eat whatever he wants. Only he has to kiss girls sometimes. Gross! And my dad's even more grown up and he gets to watch all the TV he wants! Plus he has lots of money. More than me. But he has to go to work every day to get it. And then he has to give most of it to Mom, and some to Scott, and some to me, and take out the trash and kill bugs. *(Beat.)* Well, there's Grandpa. He's so grown up he can barely walk! *(Beat.)* Maybe I'll stay my age just a little longer.

# TRADE SECRETS

Comic

*Elliot wants his friend's new game so he plots a clever trade.*

**Elliot:** Wow! That was the coolest game I ever played! I can't believe your parents bought it for you. You are so lucky! All I have are ancient games like Scrabble and Yatzee. *(He makes a "Blah" face.)* Whoopee. I want this game so bad! Hey, Greg, how about I trade you something for your game? You can have my Hot Wheels? *(Beat.)* Well, how about my baseball cards? *(Beat.)* C'mon! Wait, I've got it. I'll trade you my little sister? *(Beat.)* It's perfect! If you want lots of new games. Look, my parents won't buy this game for me even though they have lots of money. So. . . I'll take yours, you take my sister, and then I'll go home and say, "Hey, has anyone seen Chelsey?" They'll go crazy and start to panic. Just then, you call and disguise your voice and say, "If you want Chelsey back, you have to give me $5,000 or else. . . or else. . .or else I'll adopt her!" *(Beat.)* Don't worry, they'll definitely want her back. Trust me. They like her.

# THE WHEELBARROW NIGHTMARE

Comic

*Frank tells his older sister about an embarrassing experience at the school picnic.*

**Frank:** I'm never leaving our house again! *(Beat.)* Because we had all kinds of races and an obstacle course today. And I got picked for the wheelbarrow race. But they stuck me with Bobby Bigelow. He's so slow. So I said I'd do the wheelbarrow and he'd hold my legs. When they said "Go!" I took off really fast and Bobby was trying to hold on around my ankles, but he wasn't going as fast as me. Then he almost dropped me but he grabbed on to the bottom of my jeans. I was crawling on my hands so hard that suddenly, my jeans slid down to my knees! Everyone started laughing! Even Bobby! Oh, and, of course, I was wearing Freddy's Barney underwear because I couldn't find any clean ones this morning. It was awful! I won the prize — like I really wanted it after that! Now everyone's gonna tease me forever. I hope when they do tug-of-war, that Bobby Bigelow is in the front near the mud pile!

# BULLY BOY

**Comic**

*Kevin teases his younger brother about having a crush on a girl.*

**Kevin:** Hey, Billy, where are you? Would you just come out already? Come on. You're my little bro. I was just kidding around. I know you can hear me! All right, look, I promise I will never ever tease you about Jenny again. Girls are cool. I'm glad you found a girl you really like. Billy? I'm sorry, okay? I mean it. *(Beat.)* So there you are. You had me worried. I bet Mom will be worried too when I tell her you're in looooovvvveee! Billy's got a crush on Jennnnnny! Nah, nah, na-na — Mom!?! I, uh. . .found Billy.

# WHO NEEDS A VALENTINE?

Comic

*Joel tries to convince his friend that Valentine's Day is for dorks.*

**Joel:** Valentine's Day is really dumb, Ricky. First, you have to buy cards and write mushy, gross things like "I love you" on them. Then you have to buy chocolate hearts or candy hearts with words that say "be mine" or "kiss me." Barf! And then you have to give it to the girl you like and you don't have any allowance or candy left for you! *(Beat.)* Well go ahead if you want to be dorky and broke. Who are you going to give it to anyway? *(Beat.)* Brittany?! Do it and die, love hog!

# Boys'
# Dramatic Monologues

# FEARING PUNISHMENT

**Dramatic**

*Troy shares a terrible nightmare with his brother.*

**Troy:** Calvin, are you awake? Calvin? *(Beat.)* I had a real scary dream and now I can't sleep. I dreamed that I was down in a dark hole in the ground. And Mom and Dad were all the way at the top. And there were bugs and snakes all around and I was yelling so loud to get me out! And Mom smiled and threw my pillow and blanket down the hole on top of me. Then they laughed and went home and left me down there! With the snakes and mice and bugs and, and. . . I didn't mean to break Mom's lamp. It was an accident! I was trying to reach for the phone and the lamp got knocked over. What do you think they're gonna do to punish me? I hope it's not real bad. You'll stick up for me, won't you Calvin?

# PICKING TEAMS

Dramatic

*Jeremy admits to his teacher how hard it is to be the last one picked.*

**Jeremy:** I don't want to play, Mr. Cooper. I'll just watch. *(Beat.)* Because every time we pick teams, I'm the last one to get picked. Always. And they still don't want me on their team because they say, "You can have him — no, you take him." So forget it — I'm not gonna play. *(Beat.)* I don't want you to make them have to pick me. Then they'll still make faces behind my back. Why don't we ever have a math contest and pick teams? Then everyone would want me and I wouldn't want most of them on my team. Can we do that, Mr. Cooper? Then they'll know how bad it feels not to be picked.

# PAINFUL MISTAKES

Dramatic

*Chad begs his father to help him with his homework because he is afraid of his teacher.*

**Chad:** Dad, can you help me with this homework? I need you to help me now. It's really important. Come on, Dad! It has to be 100 percent right. I don't want any mistakes! Not one! *(Beat.)* Because Mr. Stanley wants it to be perfect. He's really picky and he never gives anything higher than a C and if I mess up he'll get really mad and he'll hit me again! *(Beat.)* Well, he didn't really hit me. He just has a little bit of a bad temper and, um, sometimes if you get the answer wrong he. . .uh, takes his ruler out and. . .I don't want to go back to his class! I'm too scared. Can't I go in another teacher's class? Please? Don't make me have to go back anymore.

# A SEPARATE FAMILY

Dramatic

*Peter tries to coax his newly married brother into continuing to live at home instead of moving away with his new wife.*

**Peter:** Why didn't you tell me? I didn't know you would have to leave. I thought you were just going away for your honeymoon. Mom told me you're moving out. Why? Why do you have to go? Why can't Susan come live with us? We can make room. I'm sure Mom will let her stay. Who's gonna take care of Max? And what about your room? We're a family, we're supposed to be together. *(Beat.)* You already have a family — why do you want to start a new one? *(Beat.)* Well, then getting married is stupid! It just means you leave everybody you're supposed to love. Now none of us will ever be together like this again. Please don't go away. Who's going to play catch with me if you leave?

# SECRETS ABOUT DAD

**Dramatic**

*Carl was picked up by a social worker or police officer after a concerned neighbor reported trouble at his household. Here, Carl tries to cover for his abusive father.*

**Carl:** Do I get to go home now? *(Beat.)* But Lady, I told you everything was okay. My dad didn't mean to get mad. It was my fault. He wanted to be left alone and I went in the room to get a pencil to do my homework. I shouldn't have bothered him. That's why he made me stay outside in the snow. He probably forgot that I was still out there when he left. I know he was gonna let me back in. He tells me all the time if I'd behave he wouldn't have to hit — *(Seeing her look at a bruise on his arm.)* he didn't do this, I fell down when I was playing. It doesn't really hurt anyway. Lady, I have to go. My dad's gonna think bad things — like I ran away from home. I wish my neighbor never called you. My dad always says people need to mind their own business. So can I go now? *(Beat.)* I can't stay! I can't! Don't you get it? The longer I'm here the more he's gonna hurt me! I have to go back now before it gets worse!

# FAMILY PICTURE

Dramatic

*Andrew questions his mother about the father who has abandoned them.*

**Andrew:** I threw it out. It was a stupid picture anyway, Mom. Miss Brown wanted us to draw a picture of our family. So I drew you and me sitting on a bench at the playground. Everyone had to go up in front of the class and show their picture. When I went, Darren Cook said, "Where's your dad?" Then a bunch of kids said, "Yeah, yeah, where is he?" And Jimmy Franklin said, "He probably collects trash or lives in jail." Everybody laughed. Then Kylon said, "I bet he ran away from you, or maybe he's dead." Miss Brown told me I could sit down. So I ripped up my dumb picture and threw it away. Why didn't Dad want to stay with us? Didn't he even want to meet me to see if he'd like me? I bet I'd like him. Why'd he go away? Why, Mom?

# BREAKFASTS WITH MA

Dramatic

*Terry tries to comfort his mother after learning that her boyfriend has just left them.*

**Terry:** Ma, wake up! It's time to wake — Ma, what's wrong? *(Beat.)* If nothing's wrong then why are you crying? *(Beat.)* Warren left? Where did he go? Did he leave for good, like Dad did? *(Beat.)* Don't cry, Ma. It's okay. We don't need him around. 'Cause if he really loved us, he wouldn't have left. You always tell me if somebody doesn't want to be my friend, it's their loss. Well, I guess he lost out two times then. Ma, it makes my stomach hurt when you cry. I love you and *I'm* not going to leave you. As long as we're together everything will be okay. We don't need anyone else. They just mess things up. It'll be better this way. Just you and me.

# RUNNING AWAY

Dramatic

*Mark feels ignored by his mother and reveals to his dog his plan to run away.*

**Mark:** I wish I could go somewhere far away. Not that Mom would even notice. She's too busy with all her boyfriends. Different ones all the time. And she always yells at me to be nice to them. Why should I? They're not nice to me. Russell gives me money, but it's only so I'll go get candy and leave them alone. Most of the time Mom doesn't even take me to school anymore. Miss Joyce called a lady who told Mom she might take me away if Mom didn't take care of me better. Mom just told her to leave, but she still doesn't take me to school hardly ever. I don't care anyway because I'm gonna run away. Then she'll be sorry. She'll cry so hard when I'm gone. But it will be too late. Because I'm never coming back. You'll come with me, won't you Rusty?

# THE BOY CAN SING

**Dramatic**

*Duncan explains to his teacher why he must quit singing in the choir.*

**Duncan:** Mrs. Ryan? Can I talk to you for a minute? I'm really sorry, but I'm gonna have to quit singing in the choir. *(Beat.)* Because. . .um, because all of my friends keep teasing me. They say if I'm in the choir, then I must be gay. They call me names like fag and stuff. Jarred doesn't even want to hang around with me anymore. He said everyone would think he was gay too if he was friends with me. I don't want to quit, but I don't want to lose all my friends. Maybe I could take soccer or track instead. I guess it wouldn't be so bad. But you know. . .I don't really want to. I like choir. It's not fair. How come my friends can do what *they* want, but if *I* do, I get teased? *(Beat.)* You know what, you're right. If they want to be my friends they should like me for who I am. Besides, choir is cool.

# GAME OVER

Dramatic

*Jonathan apologizes to his father for not wanting to play soccer anymore.*

**Jonathan:** I'm sorry I didn't score any goals, Dad. It's hard because everyone is taller than me and they have longer legs. I'll score one next time. *(Beat.)* I *know* I have to practice every day if I wanna be really good. *(Beat.)* Dad? What if I'm not good no matter how much I practice? What if I never score any goals? *(Beat.)* I know you think I can, but what if. . .what if I don't want to? I mean, I know how much you love soccer and that you want me to be the best on the team, so I keep on playing — because I want you to be proud of me. But I don't really want to play soccer anymore. I know *you* like it, but I don't. I'm sorry, Dad, but I'm gonna quit the team. I hope some day you can forgive me.

# DREAMING OF EMILY

**Dramatic**

*Jeff tells his older sister (or brother) about a girl he really likes.*

**Jeff:** If I tell you what's wrong, do you promise not to laugh? *(Beat.)* Okay. There's this girl in my class named Emily and I like her a lot. She's really pretty and popular, but she hangs out with Sean Phillips all the time. I saw them kiss before. And he's a stuck-up jerk. He makes fun of everyone like he's so cool. When Emily's not around him, she always talks to me. But as soon as Sean comes around, he pulls her away and tells me to get lost. I wish I was as popular as him so I could tell him off. Well, today I finally asked Emily if she wanted to go out with me. She said she only liked me as a friend. *(Beat.)* Do you think I'm a dork? I mean, do you think any girl will ever want to be my girlfriend?

# DROWNING SORROWS

Dramatic

*Derrick begs his dad to stop drinking and get his act together.*

**Derrick:** Dad. Dad, wake up! I'm starvin'. There's nothin' in the fridge again. Look at this place. We live in a pit. I don't even want my friends comin' over. Dad, you've gotta quit gettin' drunk all the time. We can't keep livin' like this. I need you to look out for me sometimes, but I'm always the one havin' to take care of you. Dad, Mom called today. She said she's gonna get her lawyer to make me come live with her. *(Beat.)* Did you hear me? They're gonna take me away! I don't wanna live with Mom. I wanna live with you. You have to stop drinkin', Dad! I don't know how, but this time you just have to.

# MORE THAN FRIENDS

**Dramatic**

*Brendan asks his best friend if she will go to the dance with him.*

**Brendan:** C'mon, Lauren. Tell me why you're so happy. Did you get the new CD you wanted? Are you going on a cool trip somewhere? *(Beat.)* I give up — tell me. *(Beat.)* Philip asked you to the dance? Wow, that's uh. . .I didn't think he'd. . . I thought he'd ask Kerri. Are you gonna go with him? *(Beat.)* Oh. *(Beat.)* Nothing's wrong. I'm just, um, well. . .I, uh. . . I was kind of hoping that you would. . .ya know. . .that you would maybe want to go with me. I know we're almost best friends and all, but I've liked you for a long time and, well, you're really pretty. Please tell Philip you can't go with him, and come to the dance with me instead?

# ASKING FOR TROUBLE

Dramatic

*Eddie urges his friend not to carry a gun to school.*

**Eddie:** Man, I don't know about this. I don't think it's such a good idea. What if you get busted? If they find out you're carrying a gun in school, you could get in serious trouble. *(Beat.)* I'm not chicken! Look, I've done everything in the past: breaking into that old house, taking beer from the fridge, stealing smokes at the store. We've had so much fun. Why can't we keep it that way, without a gun? What if it accidentally goes off and you kill somebody? You can kiss your life good-bye. They'll lock you up and forget all about you. Trust me. That's what happened to my dad. He went to jail and he never came out. Accident or no accident, it doesn't matter. It still ends the same way. So if you take that gun to school, I'm out. I mean we're not friends anymore. *(Pause.)* So, what's it gonna be?

# OUTSIDE DAD'S FOOTSTEPS

Dramatic

*Adam tries to make his dad understand that he needs to live his own life.*

**Adam:** I got a "C" on my math test. That's not so bad. It's average, Dad. *(Beat.)* But it's really hard for me right now. I have tons of homework, band practice, karate, and rehearsal for the play every night. That's a lot of stuff. *(Beat.)* I know good grades are important, but so is everything else. I'm trying as hard as I can. What am I supposed to do? *(Beat.)* Quit the play?! No, that's not fair! We're already in the third week of rehearsal and I've got the lead role. I can't quit now. Dad, I know you got bad grades when you were in school and you don't want me to do the same thing. But don't you see? You're trying to make me be perfect because you weren't. It's like I'm supposed to make up for your life. Well this is *my* life. And I'm not perfect, Dad. I never will be. Acting is the one thing that really makes me happy. I'm going to pass all of my classes. Just not with straight A's. That doesn't make me a failure, Dad. And it doesn't make *you* one either.

Award winner: Drama Monologue Competition, International Modeling & Talent Association, Los Angeles 2000 Convention.

# Girls' or Boys'
# Comic Monologues

# THE CEREAL THIEF

**Comic, Girl/Boy**

*Jessie scolds his/her dad for eating all the good cereal.*

**Jessie:** Dad! You ate all my cereal again! Mom bought this for me. See, it says, "For kids." You're supposed to eat your gross grown-up food for breakfast. Oh, no! You messed up the puzzles on the back again! The bear has to go *through* the maze, he can't go *around* it! And a bear's favorite thing is not football! It's honey, Dad. *(Calling out.)* Mom! Mom! Dad ate all the — wow, five dollars! Thanks Dad! Want some more cereal?

# THE BABYSITTER

Comic, Girl/Boy

*Nicky tries to get his/her parents to go out so he/she can hang out with the cool babysitter again.*

**Nicky:** Mom, I think you and Dad should go out tonight. Then Linda can come back and babysit! I didn't even get sad when you left 'cause Linda let me play my favorite songs and watch TV at the same time! And she said I could have one snack, but I couldn't decide between a Poptart, a dough-nut, or cookies. So she put them all on a plate and said it was one snack plate! And when I threw up later she didn't even get mad! She just said not to tell — oops! Anyway, I like her a lot. And her boyfriend, Bobby, and her other friends that came over too! They brought apple juice to drink. But they poured it in tiny glasses and gulped it down real fast like this. *(Demonstrates.)* It made them laugh so hard that they danced all over the living room — even on the new couch! It was the most fun ever! *(Beat.)* Mom, are you okay?

# GOTTA GOB?

Comic, Girl/Boy

*Shawn tries to coax Brian into giving her/him a piece of gum.*

**Shawn:** Hi Brian. Wow, look at all that gum you have! I bet it tastes good. Megan told me you gave her some. That was really nice of you. You know, if I had tons of gum like you, I would share it with all my friends. Well, not *all* of them. Just the ones I like the most. Like you. Mmm, that smells like grape. That's my favorite! My mom never buys me gum anymore. She says all my teeth will fall out if I keep chewing it. I think she might be wrong 'cause you're chewing tons and tons of gum and your teeth haven't busted out yet. You're soooo lucky. You have every kind of gum in the world. And I have none. *(Beat.)* For me? Wow! And I didn't even ask, but I'll take it!

# THE MONSTER UNDER THE BED

Comic, Girl/Boy

*Jamie plots with Joey to get rid of the monster under the bed.*

**Jamie:** Shhh. It's under the bed. I'm really, completely serious. That's why it's dark in here. Watch out! That was my knock-em-sock-em doll. It's okay if you knocked the head off. That's supposed to happen. Listen, I gotta get rid of the monster myself because my mom doesn't believe me. *(Points.)* See that stupid Barney night-light? She thinks that scared it off already. Of course, I heard the monster laughing at it the other night. You know, like *(Imitates evil laugh.)* But I've got a plan, Joey, and I need your help. The monster lives in the space between the bed and the floor. If there is no space, then there is no monster. Got it? Good. Now, stand up on the bed with me. This is for a good cause. Remember, we're stronger than the bed frame. All right. . . ready. . .set. . .JUMMM — *(Starts to jump, but stops.)* Hi Mom.

Award winner: Comedy Monologue Competition, International Modeling & Talent Association, New York 1998 Convention.

# REINVENTING TIME

Comic, Girl/Boy

*Tracy explains to his/her mother why he/she should be allowed to stay up late.*

**Tracy:** Mom, I know I'm up late, but I have a really good reason. Remember last week when we were getting ready to go to Six Flags Great America? I asked you how much longer you'd be and you said, "Just a minute." I watched the clock and you took sixteen minutes. Then yesterday when I was starving for dinner, I asked you when it would be ready, and you said, "In a minute." That was fourteen minutes. And today when you were on the computer and I wanted to use it, you told me you'd only be a minute. It took you eighteen minutes. Well, tonight when you said it was bedtime, I asked if I could stay up a little longer and you said, "Okay, just for a few minutes." So I figured I had about an hour.

# LATE PASS

Comic, Girl/Boy

*Tori tells his/her teacher why he/she is so late for class.*

**Tori:** Sorry I'm late Mrs. Applebee, but I have a really good reason. See, my alarm clock broke and didn't wake me up. It was bound to happen sooner or later. Anyway, by the time I got up, my mom had left for work thinking I was already on the bus. She's blind as a bat without her glasses in the morning. But when I got up and looked at my mom's clock — ahhhh! I already missed the bus! I had to rush and take a shower because my dog drooled all over me in my sleep. But the shower wasn't working! So I had to go outside in my pajamas and hose myself down. Then I couldn't find any clean clothes, so I had to wear my big brother's overalls. I grabbed my piggy bank — phew — lunch money! As I was running to school, I tripped five times on my pants. Then some bullies came running after me — I pulled up my pant legs and ran like the wind. And here I am. *(Beat.)* I hope I didn't miss the test.

# THE WALL OF VAN GOGH

Comic, Girl/Boy

*Brianna/Brian relates her/his calling to be a painter.*

**Brianna/Brian:** I am a very talented painter. An artiste. I am going to be as famous as Van Gogh one day. It was clear to me from a very early age. When I got my first paint set and that little brush in my hand, I knew I was inspired. My bedroom wall, like a giant white canvas, was calling to me. "Paint me! Paint me!" it pleaded. Before I knew what was happening, my hand was swirling and stroking and speckling all over! When I finished, I stepped back to admire my masterpiece. It was divine! I called for my mom. I was sure she'd instantly enroll me in the finest art school in the country. She came running into the room, and when she saw my exquisite mural, she screamed at the top of her lungs and threatened to ground me for life! No wonder Van Gogh cut off his ear! Being a naturally gifted artist is not easy in a world full of moms.

Award winner: Comedy Monologue Competition, International Modeling & Talent Association, New York 1998 & Los Angeles 1999 Conventions.

# Girls' or Boys'
# Dramatic Monologues

# PING PONG

**Dramatic, Girl/Boy**

*Adrian tries to convince his/her dad to come home and get back together with his/her mom.*

**Adrian:** Because I don't like being here. I don't mean with you, Dad. I don't like this apartment. It gives me the creeps. I want us to do fun stuff on the weekends — with Mom too. I know you and Mom had a big fight. I heard you yelling. But you always tell me that people make mistakes, and if you really care about them, it's worth making up. So, I have a great idea! There's still tons of room in the house. You could bring Mom some flowers and tell her you're really sorry. And then you could move back in and it would be just like before! We could all laugh and play together and . . .Why not? I know Mom will forgive you. Don't you wanna make up? Aren't you lonely here? Dad, if I did something wrong, I didn't mean to. Please come home. Don't you love me anymore?

Award winner: Drama Monologue Competition, International Modeling & Talent Association, New York 1999 & Los Angeles 2000 Conventions.

# MOVING AWAY

Dramatic, Girl/Boy

*Shane discovers that her/his best friend is moving and begs her/him to stay.*

**Shane:** Wow. You're lucky you get to go to Boston. I never get to go anywhere except my room. We went to Disney World once when I was little, but I don't remember going. My mom told me. When are you coming back? *(Beat.)* Never?! You mean you're moving away? But you can't! You're my best friend! You've gotta stay here. Who am I gonna play with and go to school with and ride bikes with? No, it's not fair. I won't let you go. Maybe you can live at my house. Ask your dad — I know my mom will say okay. Don't go! I'll die! Promise me you won't leave! Please?

# ANOTHER WOMAN

**Dramatic, Girl/Boy**

*Alex scolds his/her dad for kissing a woman and cheating on her/his mom.*

**Alex:** You kissed her! I saw you outside, Dad! How could you do that? She's not Mom. I don't care if you and Mom are fighting — you're still supposed to be together. What would Mom think if she knew? She'd be so upset. That lady is mean. Don't you get it? She's trying to take you away from me and Mom. She doesn't even care if I'm alive. I hate her! Dad, I don't understand. Don't you love Mom anymore? She loves you. So do I. I want us to be a normal family again. Me, you and Mom. Together. I need you, Dad. Please promise me you'll never see that lady again.

## THE AUTHOR

JANET B. MILSTEIN is an actor, acting teacher, and private monologue coach. She received her MFA in Acting from Binghamton University in New York and her BA in Theater with Distinction from the University of Delaware. Janet has an extensive background in theater, having performed at numerous theaters with a variety of companies, including the Milwaukee Repertory Theater, the Organic Theater, Writers' Block at the Theatre Building, Tinfish Productions at the Athenaeum Studio Theatre, National Pastime Theater, Stage Left Theatre, Mary-Arrchie Theatre Co., the Women's Theatre Alliance at Chicago Dramatists, Theatre Q, Cafe Voltaire, and more. Janet has appeared in a number of independent films, as well as working in industrials and voice-overs.

Janet has taught acting to undergraduates at Binghamton University, to apprentices at Fort Harrod Drama Productions, and to children and adults in various acting workshops. Since 1997, she has taught acting at John Robert Powers Entertainment Company, Chicago, where she was named Best Instructor. In addition to teaching many levels of acting classes, Janet trains talent contestants for competition at the bi-annual International Modeling and Talent Association conventions in New York and Los Angeles.

Janet also works as a private acting coach in Chicago. She trains beginning and professional actors in monologues and cold readings.

This is Janet's second book. Her previous book, *The Ultimate Audition Book for Teens: 111 One-Minute Monologues*, was published by Smith and Kraus in 2000.

If you would like to contact the author, you can e-mail her at Monolog123@aol.com.